SABER-TOOTHED CATS
A First Look

HANNAH GRAMSON

Lerner Publications ◆ Minneapolis

Educator Toolbox

Reading books is a great way for kids to express what they're interested in. Before reading this title, ask the reader these questions:

- What do you think this book is about? Look at the cover for clues.
- What do you already know about saber-toothed cats?
- What do you want to learn about saber-toothed cats?

Let's Read Together

Encourage the reader to use the pictures to understand the text.

Point out when the reader successfully sounds out a word.

Praise the reader for recognizing sight words such as *like* and *had*.

TABLE OF CONTENTS

Saber-Toothed Cats 4

You Connect! 21
STEM Snapshot 22
Photo Glossary. 23
Learn More 23
Index 24

Saber-Toothed Cats

Saber-toothed cats lived about ten thousand years ago.

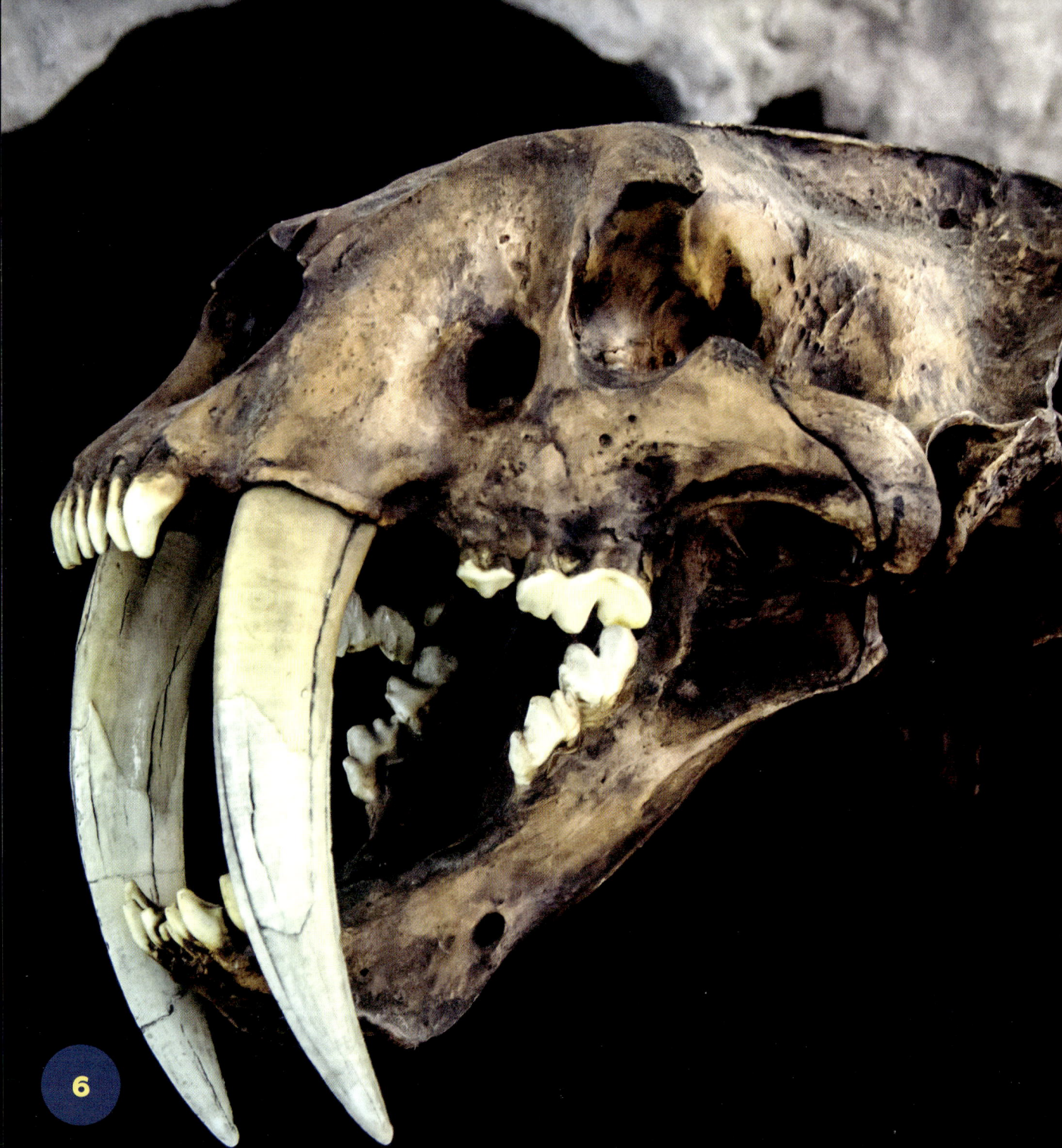

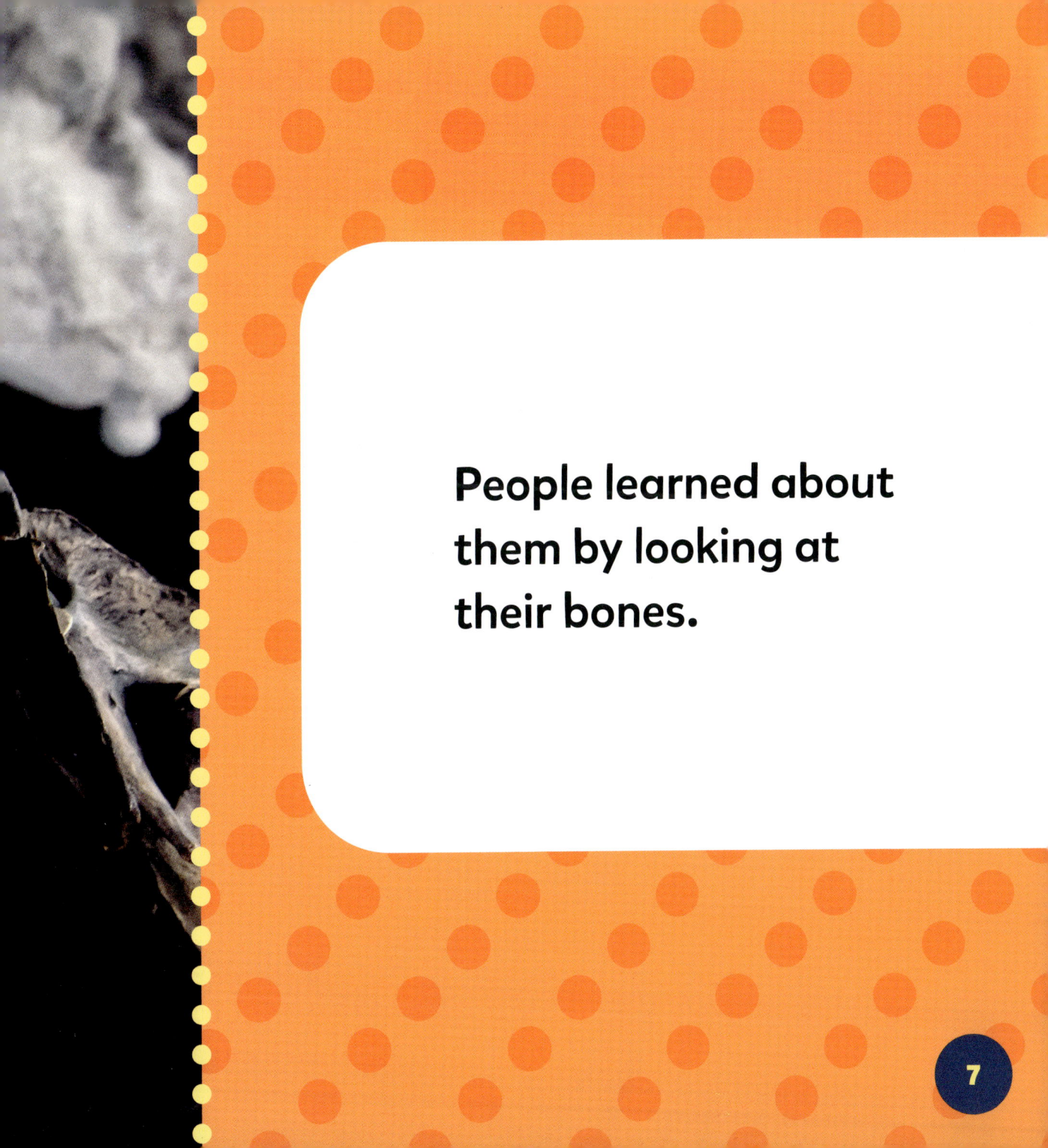

People learned about them by looking at their bones.

Saber-toothed cats looked like tigers.

They had thick fur and sharp claws.

What other animals have fur and claws?

Saber-toothed cats were about as big as tigers.

Their tails were short and round.

They had two big fangs. Each fang was about the size of a banana.

How might their fangs have been helpful?

15

Saber-toothed cats lived in grasslands. They usually lived near water.

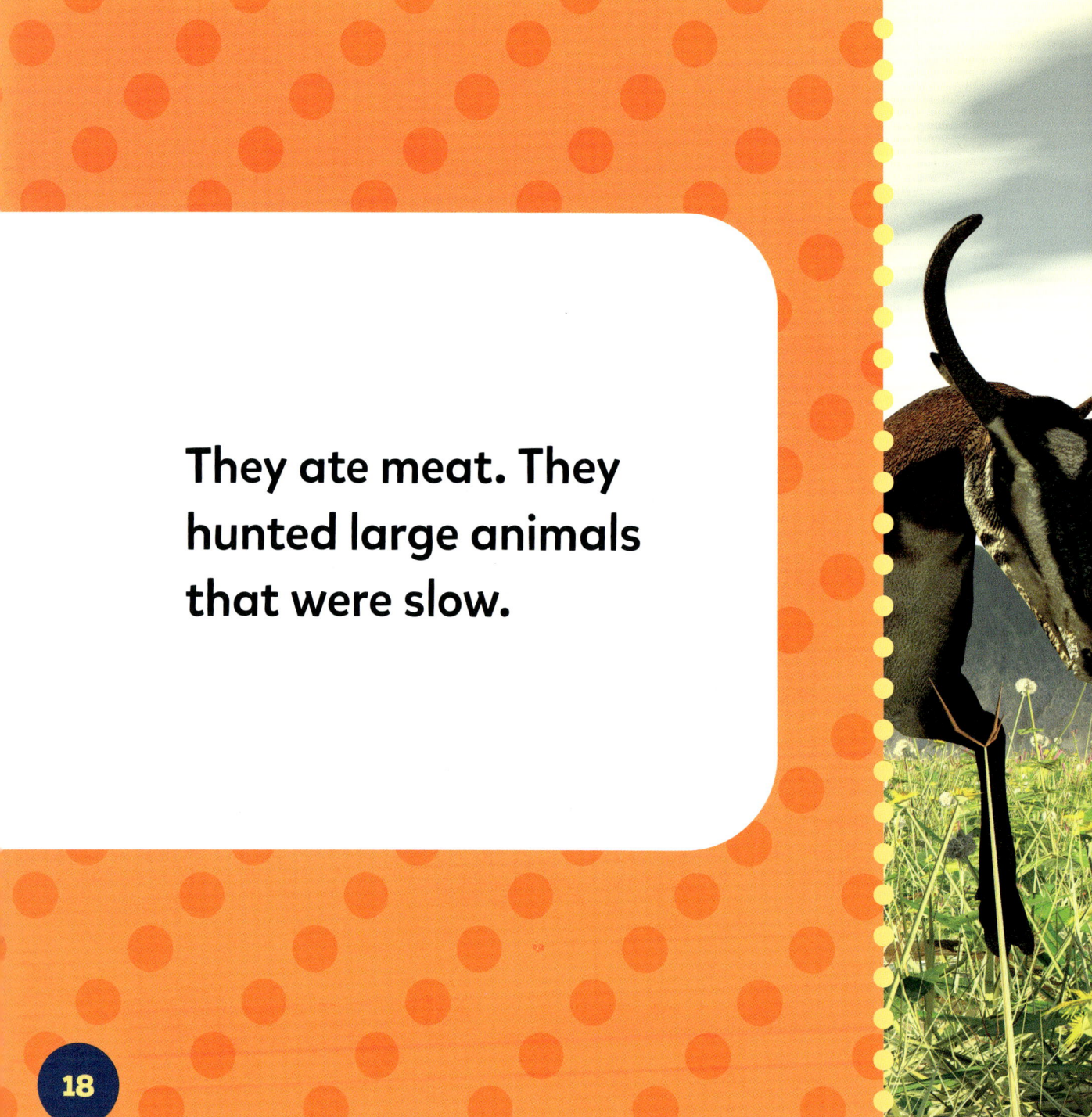

They ate meat. They hunted large animals that were slow.

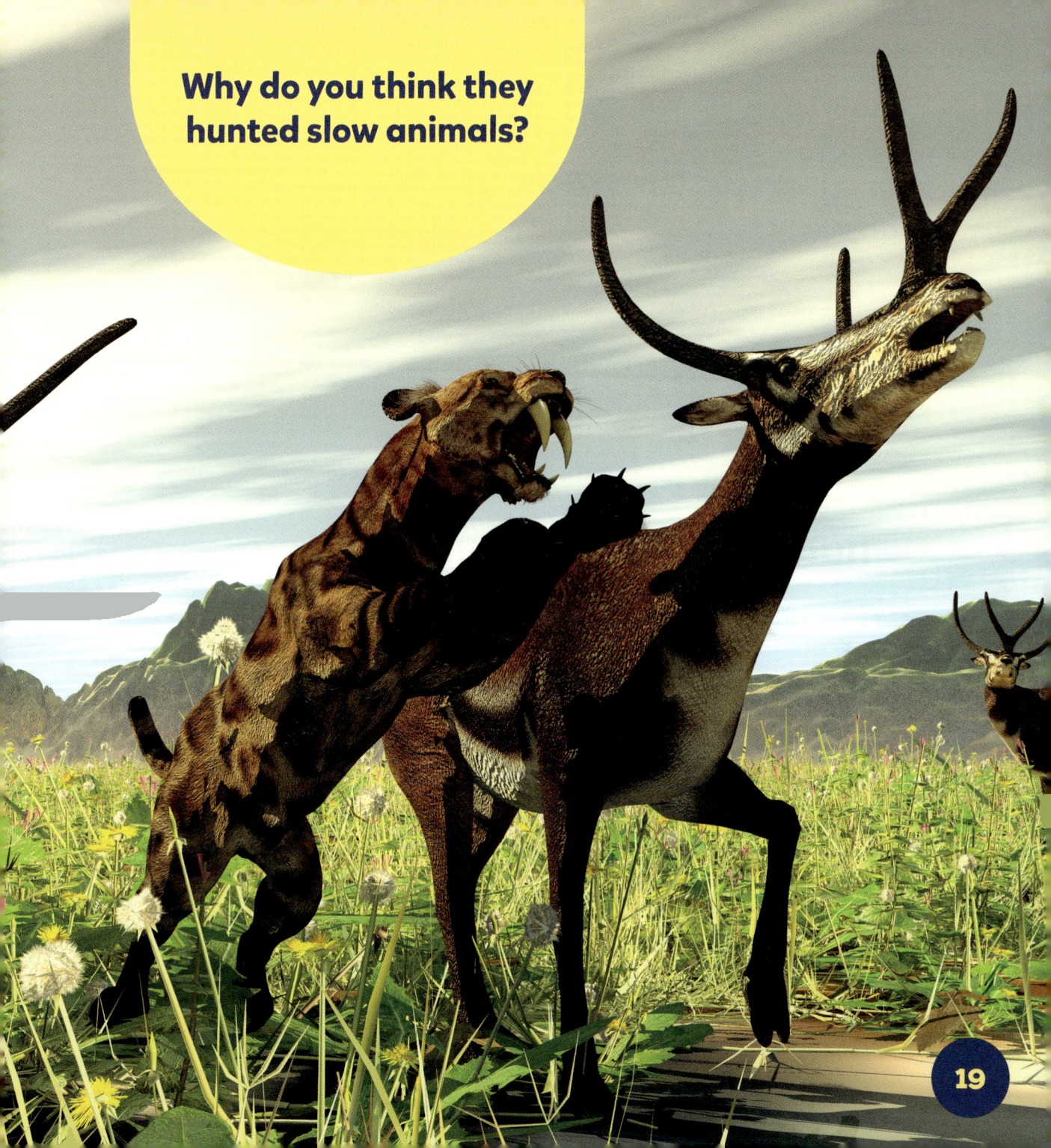

Saber-toothed cats were good hunters.

You Connect!

What do you like about saber-toothed cats?

Would you want to meet a saber-toothed cat?

What other large cats would you like to learn about?

STEM Snapshot

Encourage students to think and ask questions as scientists. Ask the reader:

What have you learned about saber-toothed cats?

What have you noticed about the way saber-toothed cats looked?

What do you still want to learn about saber-toothed cats?

Photo Glossary

Learn More

Gramson, Hannah. *Ground Sloths: A First Look*. Minneapolis: Lerner Publications, 2026.

Murray, Julie. *Fun Facts About Big Cats*. North Mankato, MN: Dash! Leveled Readers, 2022.

Murray, Julie. *Saber-Toothed Tiger*. Minneapolis: Abdo Kids, 2024.

Index

bone, 7
claw, 10
fur, 10
grassland, 16
tiger, 8, 12

Photo Acknowledgments

Image credits: Daniel Eskridge/Stocktrek Images/Getty Images, p. 5; Mardoz/Alamy, p. 6; ROMAOSLO/Getty Images, p. 8; Ondrej Prosicky/Getty Images, p. 9; Vac1/Getty Images, p. 11; Manuel ROMARIS/Getty Images, p. 12; Corey Ford/Stocktrek Images/Getty Images, p. 13; Chris Hellier/Getty Images, p. 15; Mark Stevenson/Stocktrek Images/Getty Images, p. 17; CoreyFord/Getty Images, p. 19; cloudytronics/Getty Images, p. 20.
Cover: Esther van Hulsen/Stocktrek Images/Science Source.

Copyright © 2026 by Lerner Publishing Group, Inc.

All rights reserved. International copyright secured. No part of this book may be reproduced, stored in a retrieval system, or transmitted in any form or by any means—electronic, mechanical, photocopying, recording, or otherwise—without the prior written permission of Lerner Publishing Group, Inc., except for the inclusion of brief quotations in an acknowledged review.

Lerner Publications Company
An imprint of Lerner Publishing Group, Inc.
241 First Avenue North
Minneapolis, MN 55401 USA

For reading levels and more information, look up this title at www.lernerbooks.com.

Main body text set in Mikado Medium.
Typeface provided by Hannes von Doehren.

Editor: Nicole Berglund **Photo Editor:** Nicole Berglund

Library of Congress Cataloging-in-Publication Data

Names: Gramson, Hannah, author.
Title: Saber-toothed cats : a first look / Hannah Gramson.
Description: Minneapolis : Lerner Publications, [2026] | Series: Read about prehistoric beasts (read for a better world) | Includes bibliographical references and index. | Audience: Ages 5–8 | Audience: Grades K–1 | Summary: "Saber-toothed cats had giant teeth and lived thousands of years ago. Readers learn about these fascinating cats, from what they ate to how large they were"— Provided by publisher.
Identifiers: LCCN 2024047633 (print) | LCCN 2024047634 (ebook) | ISBN 9798765669068 (lib. bdg.) | ISBN 9798765684702 (pbk.) | ISBN 9798765680414 (epub)
Subjects: LCSH: Saber-toothed tigers—Juvenile literature.
Classification: LCC QE882.C15 G737 2026 (print) | LCC QE882.C15 (ebook) | DDC 569/.75—dc23/eng/20250103

LC record available at https://lccn.loc.gov/2024047633
LC ebook record available at https://lccn.loc.gov/2024047634

Manufactured in the United States of America
1-1011833-53877-2/24/2025